CASTLE DUNGEONS

by
Jason Page

A Rotten Time

The lord of the castle often locked up his unfortunate enemies in the dungeons. These were dark, damp, dirty places where some prisoners were simply left to rot!

FIRST FORTS

A castle is the home of a lord or king. The first castles were built to defend local people and their land from raiders and invading armies. Over time, castles became much stronger — and much grander!

CASTLES QUIZ

What do you call the man-made mound of earth on which early castles were built?

a) a motte
b) a botte
c) a gotte

What is the water-filled ditch around a castle called?

a) a moat
b) a boat
c) a goat

What do you call a castle courtyard?

a) a mailey
b) a bailey
c) a gailey

(answers on page 32)

JUST IMAGINE...

...Attacking a castle. First you would have to get over the ditch (which would be full of water), then you would have to climb up the mound (which would be very steep and slippery), and then you would have to scale the palisade (which would be made of sharp pikes). And finally, when you got in, you would have to break into the tower – which would be full of armed guards!

NATURAL DEFENCES

Places that are hard to get to are difficult to attack. This is why many castles were built on top of high rocky hills or on islands surrounded by water.

EARTH AND WOOD

Castle-building began in around AD 800. The first castles were very simple and were made of earth and wood. They had a wooden tower surrounded by a strong wooden fence (a palisade). Usually they were built on top of a huge mound of earth which was often circled by a ditch.

SOLID STONE

From the eleventh century onwards, most castles were built of stone. Although they took longer to build, stone castle were much stronger than wooden ones. The first ones were basic square towers. But by the fifteenth century, they had become much more elaborate.

Kilchurn Castle, Scotland

KNIGHT RIDER

The lord controlled all the land around his castle for up to 15 km in every direction – that was as far as a knight could ride in a single day!

LORD'S CASTLE

WATCH OUT BELOW!

Stone battlements (known as crenellations) protected the archers on the castle walls, or they could hide behind long, thin slit windows. There were also holes in the floors above the entrance to the castle, or murder holes. These were used to drop boiling oil and burning rocks onto the unlucky soldiers below.

CASTLES QUIZ

What is a portcullis?

a) a tripwire tied across the castle gates
b) a large window through which cannons are fired
c) a strong gate that can be lowered to block an entrance

What are machicolations?

a) sentries on the lookout for enemies
b) murder holes
c) sharp metal spikes

What is an arrow loop?

a) a slit-like window through which arrows are fired
b) a curved arrow which comes back like a boomerang
c) a tall stone for archers to stand on

(answers on page 32)

RAISE THE DRAWBRIDGE

Caerphilly Castle in Wales stands in the middle of a huge, man-made lake. To enter this mighty fortress you have to cross a drawbridge. In the past, the drawbridge would have been raised to stop enemies entering. Caerphilly Castle took about three years to build and was finished in 1271.

ARMOUR PLATING

It wasn't just castles that were well-protected – soldiers had their own defences too! The first type of armour was chain mail and was made of metal rings linked together like a chain. By the 1400s, however, knights were wearing metal suits like this one. These were so heavy that the knight often had to be lifted onto his horse by a crane.

RONG DEFENCES

During the thirteenth and fourteenth centuries, castles got bigger. And as they got bigger, they got stronger! A deadly combination of drawbridges, stone walls, murder holes and arrow slits made some castles almost invincible.

Caerphilly Castle, Wales

TWICE AS EFFECTIVE

Like many other castles built at this time, Caerphilly Castle is surrounded by not one but two stone walls. The outer wall is lower than the inner one. This allowed archers on the inner wall to aim their arrows over the heads of their friends on the outer wall and fire on the attacking army.

WE SHALL NOT BE MOVED!

St John's Castle in Hampshire was successfully defended by just three knights and ten foot-soldiers during a siege in 1215!

YOU'RE SURROUNDED!

The first thing an attacking army did was to surround the castle. This was known as laying siege. It stopped reinforcements and supplies of food, fresh water and weapons reaching the people inside. However, the defenders were usually prepared with large amounts of everything they needed safely stored away. As a result, sieges could last months – even years!

The Siege of St. Elmo

DIGGING DEEP

Sometimes, instead of going over the castle walls, the attackers would dig tunnels underneath. The tunnels were held up using wooden props. Once the tunnellers had burrowed under a wall, they set fire to the props. This caused the tunnel to collapse, and the castle wall above it to fall down.

Reconstruction of a Roman catapult

LAYING SIEGE

Attacking a castle was a dangerous business. You needed special weapons, a huge army and plenty of time to spare!

MONSTER MISSILES

A catapult could launch missiles weighing up to 90 kg – that's about as heavy as you plus two of your friends.

WEAPONS OF WAR

Weapons used for attacking castles are known as siege engines. They include huge battering rams made from tree trunks for knocking down the castle gates, and tall wooden towers on wheels (called belfries) which could be pushed up against the castle walls so attacking soldiers could climb inside.

READY, AIM, FIRE!

Attackers used catapults to hurl missiles over the castle walls. They fired heavy rocks, and pots filled with burning tar called fire pots. Sometimes, human heads or dead animals were also fired into the castle. This frightened the people inside and spread disease.

CASTLES QUIZ

What is a trebuchet?

a) a large, moveable shield
b) a huge catapult
c) an armoured boat for crossing moats

What is a mantlet?

a) a large, moveable shield
b) an armoured boat for crossing moats
c) a protective glove

How did attackers usually try to get across a moat?

a) by using armoured boats
b) by filling in the moat with logs and soil
c) by using a floating wooden bridge

(answers on page 32)

CRUSADERS' CASTLES

Crusaders were Christian soldiers from Europe who went to fight in Palestine. On the way, they built some magnificent castles – and so did their Muslim enemies!

Krak des Chevaliers, Syria

HOME IMPROVEMENTS

Krak des Chevaliers in Syria was a small Muslim castle captured by a band of fierce crusaders known as the Knights Hospitaller. During the twelfth century, the new Christian owners built more defences around the castle, turning it into an impressive fortress that survived several sieges by Muslim armies.

The capture of Antioch

ARMED ADVENTURERS

The crusaders' goal was to capture the region known as the Holy Land, where Jesus had once lived, and to overthrow its Muslims rulers. Between 1096 and 1270, they organised eight major military expeditions – most of which ended in disaster!

SMOKE SCREEN

In 1099, the crusaders captured Jerusalem by catapulting burning sacks over the city's walls. This created a smoke screen, keeping the crusaders hidden while they attacked.

CASTLES QUIZ

How long did the siege of Antioch last?
a) eight days
b) eight weeks
c) eight months

Which of these English kings spent most of his reign fighting in the Holy Land?
a) Richard I
b) Richard III
c) Edward VI

What was unusual about the Children's Crusade of 1212?
a) no fighting actually took place
b) the crusaders took only children as hostages
c) most of the crusaders were under the age of 18

(answers on page 32)

SPOT THE DIFFERENCE

Muslim and Christian castles tend to look quite different. One easy way to tell them apart is to look at the central tower in the middle of the castle. If it is round, it was probably built by crusaders. If it is square or wedge-shaped, it is more likely to have been part of a Muslim castle. The two enemies soon started copying each other's castle designs and this led to castles that are a mixture.

WAITING FOR VICTORY

The first crusade was the most successful. For eight months, the crusaders besieged a heavily defended castle-city called Antioch – now part of Turkey. Eventually, a traitor inside the city opened the gates and let the crusaders in! The crusaders went on to capture Jerusalem, the most holy city of all.

KNIGHTLY GARB

Knights were the elite troops that led the castle's fighting force. Often, they had trained since childhood and were highly skilled in battle.

SHAKE A LEG

Sometimes when a knight wanted a new suit of armour, he had models of his legs made out of wax. These were then sent to the armour-maker to make sure it was a perfect fit!

DEATH BEFORE DISHONOUR

Knights were expected to live by a special code of honour. This meant being loyal to their lord, brave in battle and generous to the poor. A good knight would rather die than surrender or break the rules. In Europe, this was known as Chivalry. In Japan, samurai warriors lived by similar strict rules – but if they broke them, they were expected to kill themselves!

CASTLES QUIZ

How could you tell which side a knight was on?
a) from the shape of his helmet
b) from the coat of arms on his shield
c) from the colour of his saddle

What is a gauntlet?
a) an armoured glove
b) a helmet
c) a short metal spear

What was given to a young man when he became a knight?
a) a silver dagger
b) metal socks
c) a pair of spurs

(answers on page 32)

MADE IN JAPAN

Japanese castles were protected by warrior knights called samurai. Their swords were so sharp they could cut a man in half! Chinese soldiers were no less fearsome and, like the Samurai, wore helmets to protect themselves.

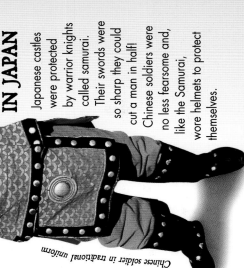

Chinese soldier in traditional uniform

LANCE-A-LOT!

European knights often fought on horseback and had many weapons. The most important was a long spear called a lance, but knights also fought using swords and axes. Another popular weapon was the mace – a studded metal ball hanging from a short wooden club.

WAR GAMES

When knights weren't at war, they still fought each other for fun. Competitions called tournaments were often held at castles. This gave the knights a chance to prove their fighting skills. One of the most popular events was jousting – trying to knock your opponent off his horse using a real lance.

II

CASTLES QUIZ

What is a manacle?

a) a chained collar that stopped prisoners escaping
b) a prisoner's simple straw bed
c) a small prison window

Which famous heroine was imprisoned at Rouen Castle in France?

a) Boudicca
b) Mary Queen of Scots
c) Joan of Arc

What was a squint?

a) a chute down which food was dropped into the dungeon
b) a small window that allowed the gaoler to spy on his prisoners
c) a dungeon's toilet

(answers on page 32)

LEFT TO ROT

The worst part of a castle's dungeon was a tiny prison cell known as an oubliette. This name comes from the French word meaning forgotten. The oubliette lived up to its name – once locked inside it, the prisoner was usually forgotten about and left to rot.

COMMON CRIMINALS

Usually, the lord of the castle only threw his personal enemies (such as traitors and rivals who wanted to overthrow him) into the dungeons. Ordinary criminals (such as thieves and murderers) were punished by being whipped, placed in the pillory or executed – to find out more just turn the page!

A dungeon in the Bastille

EVIL UNCLES

King Richard III was not very kind to his two nephews. He had them locked up in the Tower of London – one of the most famous castle prisons of them all. Shortly afterwards, the two boys disappeared and were never seen again!

DOWN IN THE DUNGEONS

Castles were designed to keep enemies out. But they also made perfect prisons for keeping enemies in.

IT'S THE PITS!

The word 'dungeon' comes from the Norman word *donjon* – meaning the main tower in a castle. In fact, prisoners were usually kept underground in the cellars, or in the pit below the drawbridge. Conditions were terrible! It was dark, damp, cold and infested with rats. Most prisoners died.

TIGHT FIT

Around 200 prisoners were once squeezed into the small dungeon at Dunnottar Castle in Scotland. It was such a squash they didn't even have room to sit down!

CASTLES QUIZ

The most serious crime of all was treason. What is treason?

a) drawing graffiti on the castle walls
b) murder
c) plotting against your ruler

Why was the letter 'M' used for branding criminals?

a) it stands for malefactor (someone who does evil)
b) it stands for murderer
c) it is a big letter which stands out

What was the punishment for being a witch?

a) being burned to death
b) being thrown off a high castle
c) spending a week in the pillory

(answers on page 32)

OFF WITH HIS HEAD!

The most common sentence handed out was death! People found guilty of theft, murder or even poaching (illegal hunting) could be killed. Condemned criminals were usually hanged but some had their heads cut off or were burned at the stake. In Turkey, anyone found guilty of treason had a knife plunged into their heart.

FANCY A DIP?

Other punishments included branding criminals with a piece of red-hot iron. Usually, the letter 'M' was burned onto the guilty person's forehead so everyone would be able to see it. The castle moat was used to punish people, too. Gossips and people who spread lies were often placed on a special ducking chair, which was then lowered into the stinking water next to the castle.

JUDGE AND JURY

In medieval times, the lord of the castle had enormous power. When a local person was accused of a crime, the lord would act as both judge and jury. He would listen to all the evidence, then decide whether the accused was guilty and what their punishment should be

CRIME AND PUNISHMENT

If you think being locked up in the castle dungeon sounds bad, just wait till you read about the other punishments on offer!

PUT IN THE PILLORY

Just outside the castle there was usually a pillory. The pillory was a wooden clamp with holes that gripped a person's head and hands. This was used to punish people who had committed minor offences – for example, shopkeepers who cheated their customers. They had to stand in the pillory all day and passers-by were allowed to throw rotten eggs and vegetables at them!

Men in pillory

PIPE DOWN

Sometimes a piper would stand next to the pillory and play the bagpipes. This would attract the attention of passers-by – and give the prisoners a splitting headache!

STORMING THE BASTILE

The story of a French king who lost a castle, then all his power, and then his head...

Storming of the Bastille

CRISIS FOR THE KING

When Louis XVI heard that the Bastille had been captured, he fled from Paris and promised to give up some of his powers. But it was too late! The revolutionaries now knew what they could achieve.

The revolution grew and soon the king lost all his powers. He was captured and was sent to the guillotine in 1793.

WHERE ARE THE OTHERS?

On 14 July 1789, a mob of revolutionaries who wanted to overthrow King Louis XVI and his government attacked the Bastille. They overran the guards and captured the fortress. However, when they threw open the doors to the cells they discovered there were only seven prisoners inside!

The cutting edge
The heavy blade was lifted using a rope. When the rope was released, the blade dropped – cutting off the head of whoever was below.

CHOP CHOP!

King Louis XVI wasn't the only person to lose his head during the French Revolution. In fact, between 1789 and 1799 more than 18,000 people were sent to the guillotine. This terrible machine was designed for chopping people's heads off cleanly and efficiently. It was still used in France until 1977!

A basket for heads

A basket would have been placed here to catch the person's head so that it didn't roll around on the floor.

Put your head here

The person to be executed lay on a wooden plank and put their head through a wooden collar. This made sure the neck was directly below the guillotine's deadly blade.

HEAD START

The guillotine was actually invented by a doctor! His name was Dr Joseph Guillotine and he came up with the idea in 1792.

Which of these people was once held prisoner at the Bastille?
a) Voltaire
b) Napoleon Bonaparte
c) Joan of Arc

King Louis XVI's wife also had her head chopped off by the revolutionaries. What was her name?
a) Louis Antoinette
b) Marie Antoinette
c) Anne Antoinette

What was the motto of the French revolutionaries?
a) Who Dares Wins
b) All For One And One For All
c) Liberty, Equality, Brotherhood

(answers on page 32)

CASTLES OF THE EAST

Osaka Castle, Japan

In the sixteenth and seventeenth centuries, fewer and fewer castles were built in Europe. However, in Japan and China it was a different story - castle-building here was just reaching it's peak!

A CUNNING PLAN

In 1615, a warlord named Ieyasu lay siege to Osaka Castle in Japan. The attack failed, so Ieyasu sent a message to the lord of the castle promising that his soldiers would leave in peace if they could fill in the moat. Hideyori, the castle's foolish lord, agreed and the moat was filled in.

True to his word, Ieyasu retreated, but then returned with an army of 250,000 warriors. This time, without the moat to protect it, the castle was easily captured!

MEGA MOAT

If you added them all together, the moats around the Imperial Palace in China would stretch for 3,290 metres – that's eight times the height of the Empire State Building in New York!

LOTS IN COMMON...

Although castles in Japan and China look very different from European castles, they have a lot in common. Like European castles, the most important building is the main tower in the middle. This is surrounded by walls often with smaller towers. Many oriental castles also had a water-filled moat – just like many European ones.

...BUT NOT THE SAME!

There are important differences too! In a Chinese or Japanese castle, only the base of the towers was made from stone. The rest of the tower was wood.

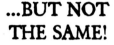
The Great Wall of China

WHAT A WALL!

The rulers of China didn't just build castles to keep invaders out. During the fifteenth century, they also built a vast wall right across northern China. Known as the Great Wall of China, it is the longest thing ever built. It stretches for 6,400 km and measures up to 11 metres high.

CASTLES QUIZ

Who lived in the Imperial Palace in China?

a) the Emperor of China
b) no one knows – it's a mystery!
c) no one—the Palace was never lived in!

Japanese knights often carried a 'mon' – what is this?

a) a badge or banner showing their coat of arms
b) a long spear
c) a small, round shield made of woven reeds

Where did the lord live in a Japanese castle?

a) at the top of the main tower
b) in the bottom of the main tower
c) next to the main entrance

(answers on page 32)

CASTLES QUIZ

Which Queen is buried at Windsor Castle?

a) Mary
b) Victoria
c) Elizabeth I

How many castles does France have?

a) about as many as Germany
b) half as many as Germany
c) twice as many as Germany

Why was the kitchen built away from the rest of the castle?

a) no one knows
b) because the kitchen was built much later
c) because of the risk of fire

(answers on page 32)

FRENCH FLYING TURRETS

A common feature of many French castles is a flying turret. This is a turret or small tower that juts out from the wall with nothing underneath it. French castles can also be recognised by the tall cone-shaped roofs on top of their towers.

GERMAN CASTLES ON THE ROCKS

There are more than 10,000 castles in Germany – that's roughly five times the number in all of Britain and Ireland put together! German castle-builders (especially in the western part of Germany) specialised in building castles on top of inaccessible rocks, making the most of the natural defences.

Egeskov Castle, Denmark

Windsor Castle, England

HOME SWEET HOME

Parts of Windsor Castle date back to the time of William the Conqueror. Many English kings and queens have made the castle their home. The current Queen and her family still stay at Windsor regularly – making it the largest castle that is still lived in anywhere in the world!

CASTLES OF THE WEST

Europe has more castles than anywhere else in the world. Not to mention some of the most unusual castles, too!

ANYONE FOR TENNIS?

The world's largest castle is Hradcany Castle in Prague, the capital of the Czech Republic. It covers more than 7 hectares – that's bigger than 270 tennis courts put together! The castle was built in the ninth century as the home of the Kings of Bohemia.

MONEY MATTERS

Building a castle wasn't cheap. King Edward I spent more than £80,000 (around £25 million today) on building new castles!

21

Because a knight's ransom was usually paid by his family, a captured knight who didn't get on with his relatives might be held hostage for a very long time indeed!

Reconstruction of man in the iron mask

MASK MYSTERY

Of course, having noble blood was no guarantee of an easy time in prison. Sometimes, it could make life even worse! One poor prisoner, locked in the Bastille in France, was forced to wear an iron mask over his head all the time. The identity of the man in the iron mask is still a mystery. However, many people think that he was the brother of the king of France and his face was kept hidden so that no one would recognise him.

RAISING THE RANSOM

A hostage would only be released if his ransom was paid in full. Sometimes, the ransom would be paid by a lord or king but usually the knight's family had to raise the money themselves.

A KING'S RANSOM

Being held prisoner in a castle didn't always mean being locked in a cold, dark dungeon. If you were important enough, you might get one of the nicer rooms!

HOSTAGE TAKING

Knights and noblemen captured in battle would often be taken back to their enemy's castle and held as hostages. Instead of being thrown into a cell, they were usually treated well. Some were even allowed to wander freely around the castle – so long as they promised not to escape!

The White Tower, London

LUXURY CELLS

Prisoners from noble families were usually treated much better than ordinary people. Often, they were given beautifully furnished rooms and were waited on by servants – even if they had been sentenced to death!

Many noble prisoners, including queens and princes, were held in the Tower of London.

CASTLES QUIZ

Which king of England was held hostage from 1192 to 1194 and released after the payment of a ransom?
a) Richard I
b) Richard II
c) Richard III

Who wrote a famous novel based on the story of the man in the iron mask?
a) Charlotte Bronte
b) Alexandre Dumas
c) Charles Dickens

Which great explorer was imprisoned in the Tower of London?
a) Sir Walter Raleigh
b) Christopher Columbus
c) Marco Polo

(answers on page 32)

TERRIBLE TORTURE

Thumbscrew

Horrible things were often done to prisoners in the castle dungeons to make them confess their crimes. Captured enemy soldiers also faced torture if they refused to reveal their army's secret plans.

A LONG STRETCH

One of the most common torture techniques was to tie a prisoner by his hands and feet to a machine known as the rack. By turning wheels on the rack, the torturers could slowly stretch their victim until he was in agony.

Torture rack

UNDER PRESSURE

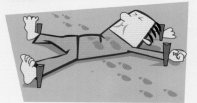

Torturers would crush people to death in the press using rocks weighing up to 320 kg – that's ten times as heavy as you!

ALL FINGERS AND THUMBS

Try gently pinching the top of your thumb where your thumb nail is. Now imagine what a thumbscrew must have felt like. The torturer would have used one to slowly crush the fingers and thumbs of his victims. Ouch!

PAINFUL DEATH

Traitors could expect an especially gruesome death. It was known as being hanged, drawn and quartered. First the prisoner was hanged from a gallows. But before he died, his body was cut open and his intestines pulled out. Finally, he was chopped into four pieces and his head placed on a spike!

PRESSED TO CONFESS

Pressing was another widely used method of torture. The prisoner would be made to lie down on the ground and heavy weights were placed on top of his body. Each day, more weight was added and he was slowly crushed to death. Pressing was usually used if someone accused of a crime refused to say whether he was innocent or guilty.

CASTLES QUIZ

Who invented the rack?

a) the ancient Egyptians
b) the ancient Romans
c) the ancient Greeks

Prisoners were sometimes placed in an iron maiden. What is this?

a) a casket filled with spikes
b) a tank filled with water
c) a room filled with snakes

A criminal's corpse was often placed in a metal cage for all to see. What was this cage called?

a) a gibbet
b) a hibbit
c) a wibbit

(answers on page 32)

25

SPANISH INQUISITION

Torture wasn't just confined to castle dungeons. At one time, even the pope approved of torture.

CASTLES QUIZ

How many non-Christians were forced to leave Spain during the years of the Inquisition?

a) 2,000
b) 20,000
c) 200,000

Which of these crimes was also investigated by the Inquisition?

a) witchcraft
b) burglary
c) parking offences

How were most heretics executed?

a) dropped in boiling oil
b) burned at the stake
c) shot with an arrow through the heart

(answers on page 32)

HUNT FOR HERETICS

In 1231, Pope Gregory IX set up a special court. Its job was to try people accused of heresy – in other words, anyone who disagreed with what the pope said. This court was known as the Inquisition and it had terrible powers.

A CASTLE FIT FOR A KING

King Philip II of Spain supported the Inquisition and encouraged its ruthless hunt for heretics. Philip also built a magnificent walled castle called El Escorial. Many kings of Spain (including Philip himself) are buried here. But this isn't the only castle for the dead – as you'll find out over the page!

THE PAIN IN SPAIN

The Inquisition in Spain was particularly ruthless. In 1483, a monk named Tomás de Torquemada became head of the Spanish Inquisition. Over the next 15 years, more than 2,000 people were sentenced to death for heresy.

ON THE RACK

Those accused of heresy were tortured by the Inquisition until they confessed. Some were stretched on a rack, while others were burned with red-hot coals. Many innocent people pleaded guilty to stop the torture.

The Inquisition

TERRIBLE TORQUEMADA

Torquemada will probably go down as one of the most evil torturers in history. Although supported by the pope at that time, he has since been condemned by the Church.

27

CASTLES OF THE DEAD

A castle was the home of a lord. But not all castles were built for living rulers!

TONS OF TREASURE

The pyramids of ancient Egypt were fortified tombs – a cross between castles and graves! They were designed to protect the spirits of the dead pharaohs (rulers). As well as a pharaoh's body (which was mummified to stop it rotting), each pyramid also contained treasures including gold and precious jewels.

GRAVE DANGER

Like many castles, the pyramids were attacked. Grave robbers tried to break into the pyramids to steal their treasure. But, just like castles, the pyramids were well defended. Deadly hidden pitfalls and traps were built into their dark passageways. The Egyptians also believed that the tombs were guarded – not by soldiers, but by gods!

DEAD IMPRESSIVE

The Great Pyramid at Giza is 147 metres high – that's more than ten times higher than the average house!

TAJ TOMB

Taj Mahal

The Taj Mahal was built in around 1650. Although it looks like a palace, it is in fact a tomb. It was built by an Indian ruler named Shah Jahan and contains his body and that of his wife. Words from the Koran (the Muslims' most holy book) are carefully carved around the edge of the building. On each corner, there is a tower known as a minaret which is more than 40 metres high.

The pyramids, Egypt

CASTLES QUIZ

When was the Great Pyramid at Giza built?

a) 4,500 years ago
b) 2,000 years ago
c) 1,000 years ago

The largest pyramid is made up of over 2 million blocks of stone. How much does each one weigh?

a) 2 kg
b) 200 kg
c) over 2,000 kg

From what sort of rock is the Taj Mahal made?

a) marble
b) chalk
c) limestone

(answers on page 32)

GIVE US A HAND

It took 20,000 workers around 30 years to build the Taj Mahal! According to legend, when the building was finished, Shah Jahan ordered that the workers have their hands cut off so they could never build anything to rival its beauty. That's thanks for you!

CASTLES QUIZ

Which of these fairytale characters lives in a castle?

a) Goldilocks
b) Little Red Riding Hood
c) Sleeping Beauty

What was King Ludwig's nickname?

a) Mad Ludwig
b) Bad Ludwig
c) Sad Ludwig

How many servants worked in Windsor Castle in the 1400s?

a) 60
b) 130
c) more than 400

(answers on page 32)

WHAT A BLAST

During the sixteenth and seventeenth centuries fewer and fewer castles were built in Europe. This was mainly due to the invention of gunpowder and new weapons of war such as the cannon. These weapons could blast through even the thickest walls, which made conquering castles much easier

CASTLE COMEBACK

However, 200 years later, castle-building took off again! In the eighteenth and nineteenth centuries, lots of new castles were built. But these castles weren't designed to withstand a siege. Instead, they were built as luxury homes for wealthy rulers. As a result, they were made to look as beautiful as possible – just like in a fairytale!

LOOPY LUDWIG

Scloss Neuschwanstein, Germany

King Ludwig II ruled Bavaria in Germany from 1864 to 1886. During that time, he spent so much money building fairytale homes (including this castle at Neuschwanstein) that people thought he had gone mad. In the end, his overspending forced the government to depose him!

FAIRYTALE CASTLES

How the story of Castle-building came to an end, only to begin again just 200 years later...

Disneyland Castle, USA

ROOM FOR ONE MORE

If you love castles, go to San Gimignano in Italy. A record-breaking 72 castles have been built in this tiny town – and 14 of them are still standing!

TAKING THE MICKEY

King Ludwig (see far left) wasn't the only person who loved fairytale castles. Walt Disney, the creator of Mickey Mouse, built a beautiful castle in the heart of his Disneyland theme park. And it was modelled on (you guessed it!) King Ludwig's castle at Neuschwanstein!

QUIZ ANSWERS:

Page 2 a, a motte; a, a moat; b, a bailey.

Page 4 c, a strong gate that can be lowered to block an entrance; b, murder holes; a, a slit-like window through which arrows are fired.

Page 7 b, a huge catapult; a, a large, moveable shield; b, by filling in the moat with logs and soil.

Page 9 c, eight months; a, Richard I; c, most of the crusaders were under the age of 18.

Page 10 b, from the coat of arms on his shield; a, an armoured glove; c, a pair of spurs.

Page 12 a, a chained collar that stopped prisoners escaping; c, Joan of Arc; b, a small window that allowed the gaoler to spy on his prisoners.

Page 14 c, plotting against your ruler; a, it stands for malefactor (someone who does evil); a, being burned to death.

Page 17 a, Voltaire; b, Marie Antoinette; c, Liberty, Equality, Brotherhood.

Page 19 a, the Emperor of China; a, a badge or banner showing their coat of arms; a, at the top of the main tower.

Page 20 b, Victoria; a, about as many as Germany; c, because of the risk of fire.

Page 23 a, Richard I; b, Alexandre Dumas; a, Sir Walter Raleigh.

Page 25 b, the ancient Romans; a, a casket filled with spikes; a, a gibbet.

Page 26 c, 200,000; a, witchcraft; b, burned at the stake.

Page 29 a, 4,500 years ago; c, over 2,000 kg; a, marble.

Page 30 c, Sleeping Beauty; a, Mad Ludwig; c, more than 400.

Acknowledgements

We would like to thank Clare Oliver, Belinda Weber
and Elizabeth Wiggans for their assistance.
Cartoons by Griff.
Copyright © 1999 *ticktock* Publishing Ltd.
First published in Great Britain by ticktock Publishing Ltd.,
The Offices in the Square, Hadlow, Tonbridge, Kent TN11 0DD, Great Britain.
A CIP catalogue record for this book is available from the British Library.

ISBN 1 86007 127 9

Picture Credits: t = top, b = bottom, c = centre, l = left, r=right, OFC = outside front cover, OBC = outside back cover, IFC = inside front cover

AKG Photo; 26/27, 26t. Ann Ronan @ Image Select; 6c. Architectural Association; 8/9c. Corbis; IFC, 7b, 12/13b, 18/19, 24/25. e.t Archive; 8/9b, 14/15c, 14/15b, 16c. Giraudon; 16/17. Image select; 4/5, 28/29t, 30/31, 30t. Royal Armouries; 25t. Spectrum Colour Library; 22/23. The Kobal Collection; 22. The London Dungeon; 12/13. Tony Stone; OFC, 4b, 10b, 11, 19t, 20/21, 20b, 28/29b,

Picture research by Image Select. Printed in Hong Kong.